In The Presence of Women the Question Is Asked, "Are Women Natural Allies?"

In The Presence of Women the Question Is Asked, "Are Women Natural Allies?"

AND WHY SHOULD WE CARE?

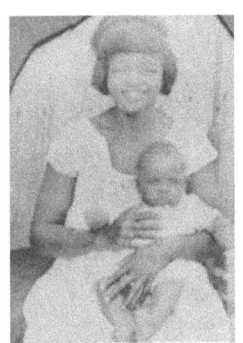 

Lorene Garrett-Browder

ISBN: 1514104628
ISBN 13: 9781514104620

*To all the women I call sisters, friends, and allies who
are woven into the tapestry of my life*

As women and girls, we carry the seeds of the past, present, and future. What will be the cost to us if we ignore each other's tears and sorrows through fear, jealousy, ignorance, criticism, and misunderstanding? If we deny our connections to each other and kill the spirit that we each bring from all the corners of the world, what will be the cost to us, to our children, to our men, and to our world?

Our work is not to inflate or deflate ourselves. It is to shed what does not work in our lives, to balance the feminine, and to release anger, fear, and jealousy. To honor the right of each of us to be, and to make space for others to enter our lives. To respect the children of others as much as our own and to believe that all accomplishments and all individuals are important to society. To let go of what does not serve us and to acknowledge and to bear witness to what is real and not an illusion. We are the change that we have been waiting for.

As women, we must decide whether we are to be carriers of hate and distrust or carriers of insight and change. What will be our decision?

Contents

Introduction

MY INTENT IN WRITING THIS book is to speak to the hearts, minds, and souls of women and girls; to speak to the wounds that life sometimes brings; and to speak to the joy and love for life that are found in relationships, families, friends, and ultimately ourselves.

The poem below expresses my hopes for all of us as a people, as a country, and as a world, but most importantly for us as women and girls—and as women and girls of color. It also expresses my desire that we come to realize that we can change ourselves and our experiences through using the richness of our differences and the power of our commonalities.

THE LOOKING GLASS
As I look through the looking glass
I see the tears of a little girl who is
sad and crying.
The little girl is crying because she hurts,
but because she has a smile on her face
no one knows that she is in pain.
She continues to wait for someone to see her.
What she receives are confirmations
that she is not important and therefore does not exist.
She begins to believe this. Maybe she does not exist.

The little girl keeps waiting for someone to tell her
that she is real, but it never happens.
She needs to realize that she is real, vital, and important,
whether others tell her so or not. She has to realize that
she is part of all that is good and beautiful in the world.
One day the glass will break, and the little girl will walk out
and know that all she needed was within herself.
She is the cup and must fill it herself.
She is the only one who can.

We know how to care for each other. We know how to not allow another to fall. We know how to look behind and ahead for each other. We know how to ensure that none of us is left behind. We know how to hold hands and trust. We know how to look into each other's eyes and find a way through our fears, tears, losses, and pain. We know how to leave blame, judgment, and competitiveness behind. We know how to touch the deepest love and the deepest wound. We know how to use love and hope to bind us together. We know how to be the lights in our homes when fear appears. We know how to value the beauty in each other and in all things.

Let us not be afraid to walk together, although the road can be long, dusty, and paved with many detours. Let us not be distracted by the pebbles and stones that can trip us up along the way. Let us remember to learn each other's story and promise never to forget. Let us remember the courage and strength of our mothers, grandmothers, and great-grandmothers. Let us not be afraid of each other. We know each other, and we know how to move beyond our fears. We have taken this journey before, and we can take this journey again. Let us not bury our heads in the sand and pretend that what is happening around us does not affect each of us in some shape or form.

The contents of this book speak to women and girls about strength and softness, love and wisdom, limits and boundaries, fear and despair, and healing and creativity. Within the pages of this book, you will also find the medicine that can heal the fear and despair that exist among us and within us.

Women's positive energy, presence, and passion are needed now to change the negative, hate-filled language and actions that are being displayed in our communities locally and nationally. I believe that before women can become better allies, we need to have the conversations that are sometimes difficult for us to have. We need to discuss the realities of racism, sexism, homophobia, and the many other isms if we are to work together on changing stereotypes, assumptions, myths, and misinformation about each other in this country, as well as in other countries.

I also believe that it is important that we find the words to talk about how we as women and girls perpetuate abuse against each other through our denial, disrespect, silencing, blaming, excluding, controlling, and scapegoating. In having these conversations, we can begin to discuss and explore our hopes, our dreams, our pain, and our value. We can also build better relationships that promote healing, inspiration, and wellness individually and collectively.

Although these conversations may be difficult, they are important in addressing what women and girls think and feel about what is taking place in their lives and in the world, as well as in making decisions related to what they think and feel. No matter how old or how young we are as women and girls, we need each other's strength and wisdom, and we must not allow others outside ourselves to define us.

White women and girls must understand how privilege affects them, as well as how it affects women and girls of color. Women and girls of color must also admit that we don't always stand up for each other and that we must change this through our words and actions in the workplace, in our families, in our communities, and on the world stage.

I dream a dream where every individual experiences the fulfillment of his or her hopes and dreams.

CHAPTER 1

Having the Conversation: The Strength of My Mothers

MANY WOMEN IN MY LIFE have shaped my thoughts and beliefs, but the women who have had the most profound impact on my life and decisions are the two women I call "mother."

MY MOTHER

My mother, Irene, died on May 2, 2001, from a massive heart attack, leaving behind a husband, eleven adult children, twenty-four grandchildren, and seventeen great-grandchildren, who all loved her. My mother had a challenging life that began in Pine Bluff, Arkansas, on August 20, 1924. She was the daughter of a Cherokee father and a black mother. Her mother was taken away from the family when my mother was very young. My mother's parents worked on a plantation and picked cotton, as did my mother and father. My mother would say that her parents "worked from sunup to sundown." She never talked much about her life or the disparities that she experienced, but I am sure that she was very much aware of them. Her life centered on being a homemaker, wife, and mother. She was a strong and intriguing woman who never shared much about herself, but when she did share, she was painfully honest. I don't know if my mother and I were allies, but I am sure that we both understood our roles as women of color, as well as our roles as mother and daughter.

The work I do now with Women As Allies is for myself, and in my mother's name and in the names of the many mothers who give so much but go unnoticed and ask for so little. I believe we are living in times that call for women's medicine and healing. If there is to be change in the world, it will be through women and girls of color and through those who are our allies. My mother demonstrated for me how to be strong under challenging conditions, as well as how to never give up on my hopes and dreams, no matter what others may think or say about those hopes and dreams.

MOTHER

Mother, you carried me in your arms, you held me close to your breast,
and you knew what I would need to survive. You knew, as many before
you knew—mothers, grandmothers, and great-grandmothers—
that to be a woman or girl in this time would take confidence, courage,
and action. You knew nothing would be given to me and that I would
have to find my way. You knew I would need your smell, your touch,
your strength, your voice, and your look to keep me strong, because one
day you would be gone, and I would have to remember.

MY MOM TWO

The woman I call Mom Two, Connie, is the mother who took in an eighteen-year-old girl who had a smart mouth but was looking for something more to believe in. This eighteen-year-old left home and ran into the arms of this woman, a daughter of the South who was married to an Episcopal minister and had one son. This family became my second family, and I learned about myself and social justice from Mom Two, maybe more than I really wanted to know, but social justice became an issue that I would be devoted to for the rest of my life. I realize more and more as I grow older that it takes many people coming together to ensure a good quality of life for each of us. If we don't have others who are guiding us and pulling for us, we are lost. Many people in my life, like Mom Two, have believed in me and have helped and guided me in moments of heavy decisions and confusion. Mom Two never gave up on me, and she pushed me to be better than I believed that I could be. There were times when I was angry with her, but she never abandoned me, and in some moments she also pushed back.

Mom Two

Mom Two, you nurtured and guided me through the self-discovery years of my life. You gave me the tools to take risks and to make decisions for myself. You encouraged me to find the answers to the questions that troubled me rather than to ignore them because of my fears. You encouraged me to embrace the world and to know that you would be there when I returned home.

The strength of my mothers lives on in every part of my being, encouraging and inspiring me to stand up and to speak up.

CHAPTER 2

Having the Conversation: About Beginnings and Endings

I WAS BORN IN 1946 to Sterling and Irene Garrett in Wynne, Arkansaw (now spelled Arkansas). I am the oldest of eleven children born to my parents. My parents were cotton pickers who worked on a plantation in the rural South, as did their parents.

My parents left the South with my sisters and me in the 1950s, coming north to build a better life, my father would later tell us. My father worked temporary jobs until he found permanent employment with a company called Hussman Refrigeration Company, where he worked until he retired, moving through the ranks from laborer to foreman, and then to supervisor. My father was very proud of his accomplishments. Although he still lived in a time when he could be called "boy," he was a man in every other sense of the word. Although my parents had many struggles living in this new northern city called Saint Louis, Missouri, they tried to maintain their dignity and pride—sometimes successfully and at other times not so successfully.

My mother was a homemaker who maintained the household with help from my sisters and me. She loved reading detective stories and watching scary movies, as well as telling scary stories that made my sisters, brothers, and me afraid to go into our bedrooms at night.

My sisters, brothers, and I attended grade school and high school in Saint Louis. We grew up learning what parts of Saint Louis were safe and what parts were unsafe to journey into alone. My sisters, brothers, and I would tease each other by saying if you can survive in Saint Louis, you can survive anywhere, which we did. We believed that Saint Louis was a tough city to live in, especially the inner city, but we all had our dreams about what we wanted to do or be. I lived in Saint Louis until my husband and I moved to California in 1983 with our two sons. Leaving Saint Louis was difficult because I knew how heartbreaking this would be for my mother, who wanted her children to remain close.

Through the good times and the bad times, what has held my family together has been a strength that could move any mountain and a softness that could heal any wound. Historically, black families have not been seen as symbols of strength in American society, but they continue to survive under difficult circumstances, as they have done throughout history.

Sometimes in family relationships between father, mother, daughter, sister, and brother, much goes unsaid, feelings are not communicated, connections are broken, and distance is expanded. And we are left with the question "Do they really love or care about me?" My brothers live their lives differently than my sisters and I live ours, but I see us all attempting to create meaning in our lives, to find a balance between grief and joy. In our attempts to find balance, sometimes the challenges are great, but we all believe in a strong connection between us, even though distance and dialogue separate us.

Growing up, I rebelled against many things, and one of them was my mother. As the oldest of my sisters and brothers, I had expectations placed on me that I did not want to be responsible for meeting. My mother held us all very close, which I found very stifling, but it was difficult to tell my mother this. I did not understand my mother's life or her needs until I became a wife and mother myself. Then I could see her story and her experiences very clearly. I don't believe anyone in my mother's life, including my mother, ever thought about the pain or the joys in her life. I remember my mother talking about her hands—how rough and swollen they were from years of picking cotton in the South. I did not think much about it at the time, but I now realize how important the softness and appearance of women's hands are to us. My mother was attempting to share with me her feelings about losing the softness, slenderness, and femininity of her hands due to picking cotton. I believe that my mother was also attempting to share with me the loss of her youth and passion.

I believe my mother also experienced a very deep sense of loneliness, isolation, and loss, and none of us could fill it even when we tried. I did not get that message at the time, but I get it very clearly now.

My sisters, brothers, and I miss the presence of our mother. I wish I had known how sick she was the last time I saw her, but I know that we cannot predict these things. Our energy now goes toward creating the best memories we can with our father because one day he also will be gone, and we will have to remember.

We don't always realize the importance of family until we no longer have one and the members that make up that family are gone. When we lose a family member, we cry for ourselves and cry for the loss of a presence that was such an important part of our lives. I know how painful it must have been when my mother and her two brothers realized at a very early age that their mother was never coming home to them again. Their mother's fate had been determined by a woman who had power over what happened to their mother and consequently had power over my mother's family. This was a power that I believe my mother felt for the rest of her life and that she resented for making her feel powerless at the time.

My mother's mother was assaulted and stood up to a white woman who was the wife of the plantation owner for whom she worked. Due to the racism in the South during the 1930s, this woman had the power to have my grandmother institutionalized in a mental hospital for the rest her life. My grandfather had no power to prevent it.

I am so grateful that both my mother and my father were able to see their eleven children grow up and create lives for themselves, no matter how full or short their lives were and how unprepared for life and death they continue to be. And even though my siblings and I are disconnected from each other at times and sometimes remember only the pain and loss and forget the memories, the laughter, and the happy times as a family, I know that my mother and my father will live on in their children, grandchildren, and great-grandchildren. This gives me great joy because I know that love and wisdom can heal sorrow and encourage us to see the hope in the todays and tomorrows.

I remember that when my family met my husband for the first time, it was as if we had stepped into a time warp, because although my family knew about this person I was dating, they had not seen him. When they met him for the first time, my brothers and sisters stared at him as if he were an oddity. My parents were warm and welcoming but not sure what to think about this man their daughter had brought to their home. My father and mother quickly fell in love with him and could see who he was beyond the color of his white skin. He was a kind, gentle, respectful, and unassuming person, with a willingness to be open and to learn about this family. Our relationship was taking place during a time when it was against the law to marry outside your race.

As a country, we continue our attempts at legislating whom someone can love and marry, even though it is 2015 and not 1966. Today there are those who say that they want their country back and who want to legislate who has the right to be an American. I say to them that there are many who remember the pain, the bloodshed, and the inhumanity of our past and will never return to that time in our history. And because we remember our history, we know that injustice continues to survive among us and must be fought against every day. But we must also remember that hope, love, and inspiration exist among us as well.

My husband and I watch our sons and their families grow, building the lives that they want for themselves, and we know that the circle of life continues. And we know that someday we will be gone, and they will remember the love and presence that we attempted to share with them. Our hope is that they will remember in their good times and bad times the many who paved the way for them to stand, to speak, and to succeed, no matter how many more obstacles are left to combat.

As I speak of remembering, I must now speak also of grief—of the loss of our oldest son, who died September 12, 2011, from a heart attack. This tragedy threw our family into the shock, the pain, and the mourning of a life gone too soon. We grieved the loss of a man who was a son, brother, father, brother-in-law, grandson, cousin, uncle, and friend. I must speak also of the death of my father, who died October 28, 2014. He was a father, uncle, father-in-law, grandfather, and great-grandfather who lived a long life and died peacefully at eighty-six years of age.

By learning to love, honor, respect, trust, and forgive ourselves, we can then begin to address what affects our lives and how this in turn affects our relationships and our families. We can also encourage conversations that relate to how we as a people will choose to live together and share our grief and memories. And we can address how women and girls of color must be involved in this process, as well as in these conversations of life, death, and healing.

As I reflect on my family history and its high points and low points, it is clear to me that our work as women and girls of color is not to inflate or deflate ourselves. Our work is to shed what does not work in our lives, to balance the feminine, to release anger, to release fear, and to release jealousy. Our work is also to honor the right of each of us to be, to make space for others to enter our lives, and to respect the children of others as much as our own. Our work is to believe that all dreams and accomplishments are important and to acknowledge and to bear witness to what is real and not an illusion in our lives. We also need to defend and to accept our strength, our anger, and our courage and not label ourselves with anything negative. There are women who say that they speak for women and girls of color, but women and girls of color must speak up for ourselves, for our lives, and for our children's lives.

As women and girls of color, we must cultivate common ground where valuing truth, integrity, and spirit and holding world views of inclusion rather than exclusion are the norm rather than the exception. We must find common ground where we are able to stand up for others and to acknowledge their contributions and dreams without exclusion or fear, in order to restore what is our true and essential nature. We must shed people, places, and situations that do not nurture us. The belief must be that every individual is important to the whole and that our accomplishments and connections mean something; this is the glue that holds us and our families together. We must dare to be bold in this belief, because using fear, misinformation, omissions, and hate speech only creates separation and destruction for us all.

I have said many times I am not like my mother, but I discover every day how much I am like my mother. I smile because I know that I carry within me my mother's story, my father's story, my story, and the stories of my sisters and brothers, and they carry my story within them, as well as our memories and losses.

MY DREAM CONTINUES

My dream continues to be filled with hope and promise for all of the members
of my family for long and happy lives. It continues in my mother's name,
in the memory of my son's smile, and in my father's words of wisdom.
I know these are the memories that my family members and
I will all carry with us until we meet again.

IN MY MOTHER'S NAME

My mother carried me in her arms, she held me close to her breast, she
Knew what I would need to survive, and she knew as many before
her knew—mothers, grandmothers, and great-grandmothers—that to be a
woman or girl in this time would take confidence, courage, and wisdom.
She knew nothing would be given to me, and I would have to find my way
alone, unprotected, and unseen. She knew I would need her smell, her
touch, her strength, her voice, and her look to keep me strong,
because one day she would be gone, and I would have to remember.

WITH MY FATHER'S WISDOM

My father always said to my sisters, brothers, and me as we were growing up
that we should always remember who we are and where we came from and treat
ourselves and others with dignity and respect, even if dignity and respect
were not given to us in return. I carry my father's words with me always,
even at times when his words are hard to follow.

MY SON'S SMILE

My son's smile, his gray-green eyes, and the quietness of his voice. I remember
the strong determination of his heart that filled the need to take care of his
family, although his heart gave out too soon. His legacy lives on in his children,
in his family, and most of all in his brother.

*We know that the circle of life continues to inspire us to love and
to remember, although the absence of the ones we love lingers
on in our hearts.*

CHAPTER 3

Having the Conversation: My Dream

I BELIEVE THAT AT SOME stage in our lives, we all come to a point where we ask the following questions: "What is my purpose in life?" or "Am I living my dream?" or "Have I lost sight of my dream, and am I now walking in darkness without a dream?" My hope is that we never lose sight of the fact that we can change our experiences and dream a different dream, because we get to choose again and again the path for ourselves, a path that encourages us to break old patterns and to discover our own personal power and courage.

My dream is that as women and girls, we embrace our strength and our softness and not allow others to define this for us.

My dream is that as women and girls, we become secure and safe in our bodies and minds.

My dream is that as women and girls, we find peace and contentment in the fullness of our own bodies and minds, no matter our shape, size, skin color, age, religion, sexual orientation, community, or country.

My dream is that as women and girls, we understand the importance of embracing each other's story, purpose, and dream and hold them sacred.

My dream is that as women and girls, we realize that what we teach we also learn and that what we learn can sometimes be challenging but is always rewarding.

My dream is that as women and girls, we boldly claim the creativity and healing that are within us and use this gift to heal ourselves and to support others in their healing.

My dream is that as women and girls, we not allow fear and despair to keep us stuck in the past but use the past and the present to improve our future.

My dream is that as women and girls, we allow our competitiveness to give way to sharing and inclusiveness.

My dream is that as women and girls, we own our feelings and not depend on others to fill us up.

My dream is that as women and girls, we will look back over the entirety of our lives no matter what the positives or negatives were and say, "Well done."

My dream is that as women and girls, we respect our experiences mentally, emotionally, physically, and spiritually, no matter what stage of life we are experiencing.

My dream is that as women and girls, we see ourselves as healers with an inspirational presence of courage, balance, clarity, softness, wisdom, and determination.

My hope is that we never lose sight of the
fact that we can change our experiences
and dream a different dream.

CHAPTER 4

Having the Conversation: Women Realizing Our Worth and Value

I WANT TO SAY TO women and girls that it is not important how others see us, but it is important how we see ourselves. We are responsible for our lives and our actions, and we are capable of changing our experiences by healing, rejuvenating, and loving ourselves in healthy ways.

It is important that we learn to love ourselves no matter what others think or say about us and that we see the truth of who we are and understand how one person can affect another's life through words, actions, and experiences, positively or negatively.

It is important that we not become victims or victimizers, that we release the toxicity in our lives and expect good things to happen, and that this become what we manifest.

It is important that women and girls realize our worth and value in changing what is hurting us individually and collectively. Through our experiences, our words, and our actions, we can make a difference. A difference that is built on relationships that are inclusive, healing, supportive, restorative, and inspiring. A difference that encourages us to tap into the source of love that we all possess but sometimes, because of various circumstances, we are unable to express or connect to that source. We are the light bearers, we are the leaders, we are the arms and hands that support the endings, beginnings, and the in-between times of our life experiences. We must not allow others to label us with stereotypes or assumptions that attempt to place us in positions of inferiority.

We as women cannot be natural allies if we don't attempt to understand each other's history, experiences, circumstances, and story.

CHAPTER 5

Having the Conversation: Are Women Natural Allies?

I HAVE RECEIVED VARIOUS ANSWERS when I have asked the question "Are women natural allies?" Many have stated, "No, women are not natural allies," and yet others have answered yes to this question. Women and girls speak of women who gain positions of power and treat other women and girls with the same power plays that we accuse men of playing. What surprises me is that women are reported to be more vicious and competitive than males are. Women of color in positions of power have not done very well either. We get stuck in not wanting to appear to show favoritism, or we adopt an attitude along these lines: "After all, I got to where I am through hard work, and no one helped me." We forget the women who gave their lives before and during the civil rights movement, enabling us to hold the positions that we hold today, and instead we work against each other from positions of fear, manipulation, and control, repeating a history of pain, shame, and hostility.

The women's movement has long been an advocate for women and girls but not always for women and girls of color. Women who have brought issues of sexism and racism to the table have on many occasions been ostracized or isolated in the workplace and in organizations. In the workplace, women of color can be labeled *insubordinate* or any other word that signals distrust by the person in charge who feels threatened by or has assumptions about who we are or who we are not as women and girls of color. We have not established a true women's movement in this country yet, but I continue to hope that all women's and girls' concerns will become important to the women's movement.

I do not believe that women are natural allies, but I do believe that we must become better allies if we are to work together on issues that concern us. We must build relationships where we show respect for each other no matter the situation or circumstance. One important ingredient needed in building these relationships of respect is trust, trust that comes from within ourselves and allows us to decide where and with whom to place our trust without having to explain or justify our decision to anyone.

To Black Women and Other Women of Color

May you be filled with all the love that you give to others. May you always know that you are loved and that your grace is felt by many. May your heart never feel empty. May you always know how much you have touched others and that we are so grateful. May you always know that your experiences are real no matter what others tell you about your thoughts and feelings. May you be empowered to continue to move in positive ways toward your destiny as you have always done, knowing that there will be those who will stand by you and those who will not acknowledge you. As black women and women of color, you know and understand who you are. You carry your history within you.We must support each other in remembering and honoring our individual histories.

To White Women

Shall I call you sister, friend, or ally? What do we bring to each other that is real, generous, and compassionate? I believe there is a place within us where there is no misunderstanding—a place where we can come together, where we see each other and listen to each other without guilt or blame. The truth of who we are rests in you and me knowing that we are a part of each other and that we must build compassionate alliances with each other if we are to work together on issues of individual and mutual concern. I am your sister.

BEING AN ALLY

When we are willing to be open, to listen, to support, to trust, and to respect
another's experience or point of view without judgment or blame,
this is being an ally.

When we have no need to control situations, persons, or outcomes and are
willing to be wrong and to ask questions,
this is being an ally.

When we are open to learning from a variety of situations, both comfortable
and uncomfortable,
this is being an ally.

When we are open to hearing and to feeling the pain of another without
needing to understand it, fix it, or defend against it,
this is being an ally.

When we are willing to not be adversarial and to understand how privilege,
unequal access, and lack of protections affect all our lives,
this is being an ally.

When we support, respect, and encourage expressions of individual traditions, histories, struggles, and accomplishments,
this is being an ally.

When we go each day into the world with words that nourish, heal, soothe,
restore, rejuvenate, and are loving,
this is being an ally.

When we are willing to open our hearts to opportunities and possibilities,
this is being an ally.

When we are willing to understand that every life is important to the world, this is being an ally.

An ally is willing to walk in another's shoes and attempt to understand the person's path without criticism or judgment, although it may be different from her own.

STEPS IN BECOMING AN ALLY

If women are not natural allies of each other, what gets in the way? And what would it take for women to become dependable allies?

WHAT IS AN ALLY?

- someone who will speak up and stand up for you regardless of the situation or circumstance, whether you are present or not
- someone who encourages you to be your best and sees your best but accepts you at your worst

WHY BE AN ALLY?

- to learn and to build communities and relationships of trust instead of fear
- to be proactive instead of inactive or reactive when a situation presents itself
- to stand up and speak up for justice and fairness for all people
- to push ourselves to new levels of understanding and interaction with others
- to reduce conflict and isolation as part of our own growth
- to break down assumptions and to create opportunities and space for healing
- to increase intimacy and reduce vulnerability by fostering kindness rather than hate
- to make a difference on a personal and social level by being part of the solution rather than part of the problem
- to create a world where we can all live, feel safe, and have a strong impact

HOW CAN WE BE ALLIES?

- by not being complacent and by letting go of the ego
- by taking personal responsibility to face your own demons
- by taking care of yourself and by respecting another's anger
- by being the voice but also by learning how to be present and silent

- by accepting differences and addressing commonalities
- by understanding another's oppression and interrupting that oppression through action
- by validating another's truth and asking how you can support him or her
- by encouraging another to expect more and not settle for less
- by remaining hopeful
- by remembering that we live in a multicultural and multiracial world

WHAT STOPS US FROM BEING ALLIES?

- our fears
- our assumptions
- distrust and anger resulting from our own pain
- distrust and anger resulting from being silenced or blamed

It is important that we understand how the intersections of race, gender, age, class, violence, homophobia, religion, and much more converge with our assumptions and expectations to exploit, assault, diminish, and control us. Having conversations related to what an ally is, why being an ally is important, and what stops us from being dependable allies encourages us to go deeper.
It is also important to discuss the issues that make us feel uncomfortable but are necessary in our dealing honestly with each other.

CHAPTER 6

Having the Conversation: Telling the Truth

KATIE AND I HAVE BEEN friends for more than thirty years and have been each other's support system through both challenging and wonderful times. We have come to know the importance of having someone in your life who will tell you the truth no matter what but will do it in a way that is loving and caring. Katie came up with the idea of the "Women's Recovery Institute of Two" because of the support, hope, inspiration, encouragement, and communication we give to each other. We are each other's friend, sister, and ally. We are dependable, committed, and present. I believe that as women and girls, we must build relationships like this for ourselves, as well as for our own survival, mentally, emotionally, physically, and spiritually. We must build relationships where we are willing to stay with each other no matter how painful or smelly the situation is and to say "I am here with you" and "I am not going anywhere."

Katie and I act as mirrors for each other, reflecting back to each other what we see, feel, or think, including the good, the bad, and the ugly. Sometimes we like what is reflected back and sometimes we don't, but whatever is reflected back is always valuable and transformative. What we mirror for each other is that we matter, that we count, that we are seen, respected, and loved. What we validate for each other is the knowledge that we are always good enough and that there is always plenty in the world for us, no matter what. We encourage empathy and compassion for ourselves, for each other, and for others by knowing our own worth and by knowing that we are safe, secure, and protected. We support each other in understanding that our life experiences are up to us and that we can change what we don't want.

I believe that people come into our lives at just the right moments to assist us, and I am so blessed to have a friend, a sister, and an ally like Katie. She has seen me at my worst, and she has seen me at my best, and she continues to carry a vision for both of us that is abundantly and absolutely full and expansive, as I do for her.

Many other women in my life whom I call my sisters, friends, and allies have not known me as long as Katie has, but they also carry a vision of our relationship that is abundantly and absolutely full and expansive. We each know that the other is there in the good times and in the most challenging of times. We are dependable and committed to our relationship, and we trust each other with our deepest thoughts and our deepest feelings. These women have been with me through the celebrations and the losses in my life, and I hope I have done the same for them.

I am grateful for the wisdom and love of my sisters, friends, and allies!

> ***When we are open to hearing and feeling the pain of another without needing to understand it, fix it, or defend against it, this person is an ally.***

CHAPTER 7

Having the Conversation: Changing Our Lives

WOMEN AND GIRLS ARE THE mirrors that reflect one another's wounds, health, wisdom, peace, grace, beauty, courage, power, and creativity. My friends, sisters, and allies help me to remember this, and I think that I help them to do the same.

CHANGE

Change is inevitable, and therefore fighting against it drains us of the energy that we will need to master the changes that will surely come. Our life experiences are up to us, and we can change what we don't want.

Changing our lives and our experiences sometimes means standing alone, and sometimes it means having someone walk with us spiritually and physically to acknowledge that we are not alone.

Changing our lives and our experiences sometimes means knowing that we are teachers and students, and sometimes it means that we show up for ourselves first.

Changing our lives and our experiences sometimes means learning to love ourselves unconditionally and sharing with others this unconditional love, and sometimes it means being able to sit in our own stuff long enough to gain meaning even though it stinks.

Changing our lives and our experiences sometimes means surrounding ourselves with affirmations that affirm the divinity that we all possess, and sometimes it means honoring another's path, although it may be different from our own.

Changing our lives and our experiences sometimes means understanding the connection between the child within the woman and understanding the connection of the spirit who holds both the child and the woman in firm hands.

Hate does not heal our wounds or our history; only love
and understanding can do this.

The Pain behind the Mask

How shall I say I lived my life? Shall I speak of the days that filled my life with hope, or shall I speak of the pain tucked away beneath layers of anger and rage for years, decaying and growing more poisonous every day? Shall I pretend that every day I loved and was loved back? What would be the truth? Does anyone really want to hear the truth? Shall I pretend and pretend again? How shall I say I lived my life? I have often spoken of families, I have often spoken of communities, and I have often spoken of the many tomorrows to be experienced. I have often said that there is hope for all of us, but is there? Life, love, and light hold me captive to the longings for something better than the yesterdays. Why do I feel so sad? Is it because I believe there are no more tomorrows, or is it that I am afraid of the todays? When life began for me, there was so much promise, so many dreams, so much time. Where did it all go? You ask what makes me happy, and I say what makes me happy, but I am not heard, I am not seen, and I am told that I am an angry woman, too sensitive, not good enough. Must I make others comfortable and happy before I can be happy?

The answer is that I must love myself. I must get in the boat and take the journey no matter where it leads. The wounds will heal, and I will breathe again, I will see again, I will hear again, I will feel again, and I will walk with grace in the world without blame, without shame, and without fear or anger. And I will know that I have always been good enough and that I have value. The tears come so easily, and my head feels as if it is going to break into a million pieces. If I let the tears fall, will I be able to stop them? Or will I drown in them never to be found, or, at best, for it never to be known that I have drowned? I am told that gifts of the heart are important even if they are not remembered and that the pain we carry hidden behind our everyday masks is not so hidden. And I am told that we all can sense the love and the pain in another if we choose to go where it takes us, through the joys, through the losses, through the memories, and back again. And each day we begin again.

And now the healing begins.

CHAPTER 8

Having the Conversation: What We Feed Ourselves

WHAT WE FEED OURSELVES METAPHORICALLY on a daily basis in regard to relationships and situational experiences is important in developing our awareness of self and others.

Feeding ourselves food that is nourishing, healing, and loving is important. We deserve the best and must feed ourselves the best and not just consume the leftovers from everyone's plate.

Learning to love ourselves in compassionate and powerful ways can be the start of not starving ourselves emotionally, physically, mentally, and spiritually.

COMPASSION
My message is
that through openings and beginnings we can
begin to touch life and all its wonders. I ask that you
not be afraid to open with me and to embrace your expansion.
I share with you the water, which is my element,
the autumn, which is my season, the sticks and stones,
which are my instruments.
My message is about opening to new worlds,
new experiences, and new possibilities.
My silence, our silence, is about listening
to nature and to each other.

Through this listening, we come to understand each other.
We learn that when we are in our wisdom, we can be open to
compassionate outcomes for each other and that the actions we
take on behalf of each other have positive intentions,
because we approach them from
an open and full heart.

POWER

My message is
that behind all life there is death, and
behind all death there is life.
I ask that you not be afraid to dance
with me and that you embrace your fears.
I share with you the air, which is my element,
the winter, which is my season, the rattle, which is my instrument.
My message is about healing our fears.
My dance, our dance, is about our interactions together.
Through birth, death, and life, we come to understand each other.
We learn to be in our power and not in our fears.
We learn to take actions that are healing
for ourselves and each other
from a place of softness.

LOVE

My message is
that through growth and rebirth we learn
and expand who we are and who we can become.
I ask that you
not be afraid to move with me into the unknown.
I share with you the earth, which is my element,
the spring, which is my season, the drum, which is my instrument.
My message is about experiencing and joining in love.
My story, our story, is about paying attention, listening, and

experiencing together.
Through sharing our stories, we come to understand each other
and are moved to places that we have never been before.
We learn to take actions
from a place of heart, love, and wisdom.

NOURISHMENT

My message is
that in order to sustain life it must
be fed and nurtured. I ask that you
not be afraid to eat with me and nourish your body, soul, and spirit.
I share with you the fire, which is my element,
the summer, which is my season, the bell, which is my instrument.
My message is about nourishing ourselves and others.
My song, our song, is about walking healthy paths
and carrying healthy visions of each other.
We learn that the truth lies within you and me, and the actions
that we take from this truth will depend on how well
we have nourished ourselves.

*Compassion, love, nourishment, and power are important ingredients in
our daily lives and in our daily interactions with others if we are to create
healthy paths for ourselves and for others.*

CHAPTER 9

Having the Conversation: The Path of Black Women

THE WISDOM OF BLACK WOMEN and of other women of color has been expressed in scholars' prolific writings placing women and girls of color at the center of their discussion on issues of slavery, lynching, feminism, and womanist thought. Their writings have also included thoughts on sex, race, prison reform, gender, interracial relationships, homophobia, class, domestic violence, societal violence, and rape. These scholars have also placed the spotlight on the divisions between white women and women of color, our children, health care, employment, mental health, reproductive rights, discrimination, and community involvement.

We owe much gratitude to these scholars. They are showing us where we must enter and where we must speak up in this modern-day challenge for equal representation and visibility for ourselves. They remind us of the women and girls history has forgotten, known and unknown, whose voices continue to confront us and challenge us to do better, to go deeper, and to never give up our vision. We are the warriors, the teachers, and the healers; we are the medicine that is needed now to cure what continues to infect us.

Women writers and activists of color have challenged us to stand up and to speak out about our lives and our concerns in our own words and in our own voices and to change what we don't want in our lives. These inspirational women include

- Harriet Tubman
- Sojourner Truth
- Ida B. Wells
- Maria Miller Stewart
- Frances Ellen Watkins Harper
- Anna Julia Cooper
- Julia A. J. Foote
- Gertrude Bustill Mossell
- Mary Church Terrell
- Fannie Lou Hamer
- Elise Johnson McDougald
- Alice Dunbar-Nelson
- Amy Jacques Garvey
- Sadie Tanner Mossell Alexander
- Victoria Earle Matthews
- Sarah Garnet
- Mary Ann Shadd Cary
- Jane P. Merritt
- Mary McLeod Bethune
- Traci West
- Lorraine M. Gutierrez
- Aida Hurtado
- Patricia Hill Collins
- Gloria Jean Watkins (bell hooks)
- Barbara Smith
- Paula Giddings
- Beverly Guy-Sheftall
- Shirley Chisholm
- Cheryl Clarke
- Toni Morrison
- Alice Walker
- Audre Lorde

The beauty of black women and girls is not seen in society's myths and assumptions about what is desirable in terms of beauty, skin color, hair, body image, sexuality, sensuality, age, sexual orientation, language, class, religion, or gender. The myths and assumptions that society carries about us influence the lives of black women and girls, and many times it is black women and girls who carry these negative myths and assumptions about themselves. We can no longer afford to be the victims or the victimizers. We don't always see our value, strength, and worth as black women and girls, and therefore society does not see our positive qualities either. We are not seen as knowledgeable, capable, or trustworthy. We are not seen as having solutions to what torments our society. Our value, our strength, and our worth must be expressed in our own feelings, thoughts, experiences, actions, and words. We are the only ones who can speak about the daily experiences in our lives; no one else can do this for us.

When black women speak in our own words and in our own voices, it is important that we address the prevalence of discrimination, racism, sexism, classism, ageism, and homophobia experienced in women's families, organizations, associations, groups, churches, workplaces, schools, and communities. It is important that we hold accountable companies and countries that claim to be working on issues of economic and social justice as they relate to black women and girls and as they relate to women and girls of color in general around the world.

In addition, we must address the profound impact that racism, sexism, discrimination, classism, ageism, and homophobia have on the lives of women and girls of color every day in America. This impact includes poverty, oppression, violence, invisibility, and silence. This impact is being neglected, and I believe that it is important to address it. We can no longer ignore these challenges that touch the lives of so many women and girls, no matter what their occupations or situations are.

When black women speak in our own words and with our own voices, we place the focus on women and girls and specifically on women and girls of color. We start to save our own lives and become better allies for each other. Women and girls of color are not seen as competent and contributing members of our society. Negative images and stereotypes about women and girls of color violate and exploit us. The presence of women and girls of color in our society is often ignored along with our challenges, our concerns, and our histories. Our contributions are seen as marginal or not seen at all. Much more remains to be done to improve the lives of women and girls of color in America, specifically in the areas of economics, racism, sexism, violence, and poverty. The face of women's advancement and achievement in America continues to be predominately not the face of women and girls of color.

As black women and girls, our mission must be to bring women and girls of color together to create opportunities for education, dialogue, networking, healing, and action. In addition, we must build relationships of compassion, trust, and hope that will bring about an increase in individual, collective, and universal consciousness on socioeconomic and social justice issues as they relate to black women and girls and to other women and girls of color. We also invite those who are our allies to be involved in this process with us and to form allegiances and coalitions.

Our goals must be to create opportunities and space to affirm our individual selves and each other, and to understand that what happens to one of us happens to all of us, locally, nationally, and internationally.

Our objectives must be to share our experiences, to express our concerns and challenges, and to take actions that come from a place of heart and consciousness rather than from fear, arrogance, separation, or ignorance. We are living in times when all women and girls, without exception, must be welcome at the table to share their ideas, opinions, and solutions.

We must ask ourselves, "Are women natural allies?" And we must invite other women and girls of color and white women and girls to participate in the dialogue, a dialogue that is inclusive of all that confronts us and affects our everyday lives as women and girls.

We light a candle in remembrance of our mothers, grandmothers, great-grandmothers, sisters, aunts, daughters, nieces, daughters-in-law, and cousins, and all the women who have paved the way for us to be where we are today. We honor, praise, and thank them, and we ask them to open our hearts and minds so that we can continue their work and be inspired to do our own work from a position of power with wisdom and softness.

CHAPTER 10

Having the Conversation: Black Women and Health

THE HEALTH OF BLACK WOMEN and girls has not received much attention. Silently, black women and girls die from illnesses at a much higher rate than in the general population. They die of illnesses such as the following:

- heart attacks
- obesity
- lung cancer
- breast cancer
- chronic pulmonary disease
- arthritis
- autoimmune disease
- diabetes
- HIV/AIDS
- mental health conditions
- reproductive health problems
- sickle cell anemia
- high blood pressure
- depression
- sexually transmitted diseases
- smoking
- eating disorders

Black women and girls must become more informed and better advocates for ourselves and each other. By doing so, we save our own lives and can advocate for a better future for each of us.

Releasing anger and fear from our thoughts, actions, and bodies reduces medical problems and concerns. The right to have excellent health care and to be in excellent health is a right we all deserve and need; it is not something reserved for just a few of us.

Black women and black families are not always seen as possessing strength and wisdom in American society. Therefore, we are not seen as having the ability to raise responsible children and to have healthy marriages. The image continues to be one of black women raising other people's children but unable to raise their own children. Although the black male may be seen as having to struggle, the black woman is not seen at all. When white Americans think about life, love, and relationships, black women do not figure into the equation. Black women have not been asked honestly about their experiences, hopes, and dreams. Black women have not been asked what we want for ourselves, our children, or our community. Does anyone care? Another question that is not asked is, what do black women want from their relationships? And what do black women feel about the many unflattering stereotypes that we carry around with us each day, even though they do not fit?

Do black women and other women of color have each other's backs and keep each other's best interests at heart? I am not sure that we do. It feels as if we are looking on while others are drowning and yelling for help, but because they speak another language or are of another religion, belief system, skin color, sexual orientation, age, or nationality, we don't trust them. So we allow them to drown in toxic waters for very toxic reasons. And we are not talking about it. Our health and our lives depend on us changing these scenarios.

I Am Your Sister

I am your sister; do you remember me? I come to let you know how it has been for me. It has been a long time, and it has not been easy for either of us. Have you forgotten me? Do you remember our growing up together, fighting for each other, not letting anyone tear us apart? Do you remember when we ran and played together, telling each other our secrets? Did you forget me? What happened? What divided us? We do not talk anymore; we do not share secrets anymore. What happened to us? What tore us apart? Did it have to do with believing that there was not enough for each of us, or did it have to do with opportunities or beliefs? Do you remember me? You tell me I only want to cause trouble; you tell me I should just be quiet. What was it? Why did you leave me? Why do you want to silence me? Do you remember me? Do you remember what we promised? We promised that we would fight for each other together. Do you remember me?

Do you see what has happened to us, or have you decided without telling
me that we no longer share what we shared as young children and
as young women? Is the commitment and connection gone? And as women,
do we now speak of betrayal and hurt without realizing that it is you and
I who have caused this division between us and that it is you and I
who must heal this division between us?

I am your sister;
do you remember me?

CHAPTER 11

Having the Conversation: Women Working Together on Issues of Mutual Concern

OUR RELATIONSHIPS WITH EACH OTHER are sometimes destructive and self-serving instead of being inspired by gentle power and wisdom. It is important that women of color and white women improve our communication with each other and engage in dialogue that seeks to help us understand our commonalities and differences rather than deny them. It is also important to understand that our life experiences are not the same and to discuss why.

As women and girls, we don't acknowledge our own fears around discussing issues of racism, sexism, or homophobia, but it comes out in our interactions with each other in the workplace, in our schools, in our churches, in our organizations, in our communities, and in our families. Racism among women and girls of color and white women and girls is alive and well, but we are not talking about it. It is affecting us mentally, emotionally, spiritually, and physically. We must find the words to talk about our racism, sexism, and homophobia if we are to work together on changing stereotypes, assumptions, myths, and misinformation about each other in this country and in other countries.

If women and girls of all races are to work together, we must have a sense of each other's history, experiences, concerns, and challenges. And we must ask ourselves how the intersections of poverty, racism, oppression, privilege, and violence affect each of our lives. We must also understand how we perpetuate this abuse against each other by denying, disrespecting, not listening, and interrupting and how we abuse each other through silencing, blaming, gossiping, excluding, controlling, isolating, and scapegoating. We must also understand how these behaviors separate us and keep us from establishing common ground.

Our work as women and girls, regardless of our race, must be to build honest, trusting, and inclusive relationships with each other in order to work together on issues of mutual concern. Building these relationships really does matter, and the importance must not be rationalized away.

WOMEN CREATING HEALTHY RELATIONSHIPS

The question is, How do we form quality relationships with ourselves that are replicated in quality relationships with others within our families, our organizations, our schools, our churches, our workplaces, our communities, and so on? By *quality relationships*, I mean the following:

- relationships that come from a place of compassion, trust, and hope that will bring about an increase in individual, collective, and universal consciousness on social justice issues
- relationships where we listen to each other and honor and respect each other enough to allow our anger and our joy to be expressed in safe and secure ways that encourage a healing of our wounds past and present
- relationships where we learn about the experiences and concerns of other cultures, as well as seek to understand our own challenges, our own commonalities, and our own differences

In order to form quality relationships, we must learn methods that change how we dominate and oppress each other overtly and covertly through judgment, blame, lies, gossip, disrespect, unrealistic expectations, supremacy, stereotypes, ignorance, and misinformation, as well as myths that perpetuate a "them and us" attitude.

We must learn skills that encourage healthy teamwork, partnership, and collaboration.

We must learn personal and professional communication skills that actualize and celebrate all our gifts and talents in addressing the problems of discrimination, racism, sexism, classism, homophobia, violence, and the many other isms that confront us all each and every day.

We must understand the individual intersections of these isms and how they converge with our assumptions and expectations to exploit, assault, diminish, control, and ultimately destroy any possibilities of healthy communication between us.

We must understand the importance of creating relationships where women are true, dependable allies for each other and not enemies as we confront the issues and problems facing us today.

> ***Women must create relationships where we are true,***
> ***dependable allies for each other and not enemies.***

CHAPTER 12

Having the Conversation: Finding Sanctuary and Healing in the Presence of Women

WHEN WOMEN AND GIRLS GATHER, miracles happen that speak to us, change us, honor us, affirm us, and rejuvenate us. Women and girls can change the world, but we must first be willing to change ourselves and to become dependable and natural allies for ourselves and each other.

Let us become better allies by taking the following steps:

- Let us find sanctuary in the presence of women who want to hear us, to see us, and to be with us as we share our pain, joy, anger, and sorrow. Let us seek out women who are accepting, respecting, and patient and who acknowledge us without judgment, criticism, abandonment, or rejection—women who show up for each other no matter what and keep their commitments.
- Let us find sanctuary in the presence of women who want to reflect back to us our beauty, value, spirit, and wholeness. Let us seek out women who want to honor the connections between women in the past and present as we move toward our future.
- Let us find sanctuary in the presence of women who understand and acknowledge the many roles that women embrace on a daily basis. Let us seek out women who are actively overcoming barriers that separate us, by using the richness of our differences and the power of our commonalities to encourage positive interactions and dialogue, as well as prevention, wellness, and relationship building.

- Let us find sanctuary in the presence of women who understand that social, economic, and political justice for all women must mean *all* women and that "all women" must include and recognize women and girls of color and our concerns, our experiences, and our history. Let us seek out women who understand that in order to bring about change, we must be the voices of that change. Through our reverence for all women, we take responsibility for the problems that affect us and form relationships that are supportive, compassionate, and life affirming.

- Let us find sanctuary in the presence of women who are making private and public choices regarding our own abilities to change what hurts us no matter what others think or feel about us. Let us seek out women who are affirming a vision of peace, a vision where we see ourselves connected to each other through communication, inspiration, and healing, not separated by ignorance or fear.

- Let us find sanctuary in the presence of women who are seeking to understand themselves and the lives of other women locally, nationally, and internationally. Let us seek out women who believe that in telling our stories, we become more conscious and that we establish relationships where we learn about the experiences, concerns, and cultures of each other.

- Let us find sanctuary in the presence of women who want to experience the sacred presence of each other without preconceptions or expectations. Let us seek out women who are creating sacred spaces where women and girls of color and our white allies can experience healing for ourselves and support each other—spaces where we are dedicated to encouraging women and girls to be completely who they are and where we speak to each other as sister, friend, and ally.

SANCTUARY

Mom Two, you nurtured and guided me through the self-discovery years of my life.
You gave me the tools to take risks and to make decisions for myself.
You encouraged me to find the answers to the questions that troubled me rather than to ignore them because of my fears. You encouraged me to embrace the world and to know that you would be there when I returned home.
I thank you for giving me your love and sanctuary.

CHAPTER 13

Having the Conversation: Finding Common Ground

THE WELL IS A SYMBOL from ancient times when women gathered at the well to commune together and to gather water for their households. The well was seen as a source of healing and nourishment, as well as a source of deep reflection and transformation. The well that is within us does not need a label, a name, or a certain practice. All that it needs is an awareness of its presence and our connection to it.

The source of who women are resides within us. That source can be found within us at the place where

- our tears are used for healing;
- our good-byes are from the heart;
- our sadness is a time for openings, beginnings, and endings;
- our processes, slow and fast, are honored;
- our intuitive powers are valued and sought after; and
- women are the warriors, the peacemakers, and the carriers of life.

The drums are calling for us to return to the heart by remembering the well and the healing waters within.

Honoring what we take in and what we give out, as well as what we feed ourselves, will determine the quality of what we give to others. The questions we ask ourselves will determine the questions we ask others and how others are allowed to enter our lives and we theirs.

When we drink from the source within us, we learn to carry positive thoughts about ourselves and others that don't come from a place of fear or hate. And we learn not to use our assumptions, our actions, or our relationships to dominate another.

When we drink from the source within us, we learn to ask ourselves insightful questions about ourselves.

- What is missing in my relationship with self and why?
- What is missing in my relationships with other women and why?
- What value do I have as a woman and why?
- What fears do I have around other women?
- What is my greatest need as a woman?
- What is my greatest joy as a woman?
- What do I want other women to know about me?
- How would I like for other women to communicate or connect with me?
- How would I like for men to communicate with me, as well as to be allies?

How Do We Find Common Ground?

We find common ground by having conversations that explore our commonalities and our differences.

We find common ground by discovering what connects us and using this to build on what separates us.

We find common ground by actively looking at what needs to be increased or decreased in our relationships with each other in order to bring about individual, social, and political change in our lives, communities, workplaces, organizations, and in the world.

Why Women Must Explore Their Commonalities and Differences

Before women can find common ground from which to explore our commonalities and differences and address what needs to be increased or decreased in our relationships, we must look at how our strongest insecurities and fears keep us from being totally who we are. For example, many of us do not stand up for ourselves on issues that are important to us, do not stand up for others on issues that are important to them, and allow our fears and prejudices to erode our courage in uncomfortable situations. We must also realize how institutionalized racism keeps us all in a place of denial even when we implement policies to assure cultural competency and diversity but continue to practice discrimination and privilege. Discrimination and privilege are spread through racist jokes and through power plays where one has the power to demean another with words or actions that show disrespect but denies that one is racist or demeaning in one's behavior.

In a family, acceptance of each member of the family is important. We cannot accept some members and exclude others, although there are times when we have to distance ourselves from family members who are destructive in their relationships and behaviors.

CHAPTER 14

Having the Conversation: History's Messages, Past and Present

HISTORY REMINDS US THAT WE are women standing on solid ground cultivated by our mothers, grandmothers, and great-grandmothers, as well as all the women who have gone before us and paved the way. What we have forgotten is that the women who paved the way for us were not only white women but also women of color. Through sharing our experiences past, present, and future, we uncover the illusions that we carry about ourselves and others, and we become more conscious. We form a consciousness that supports us in seeing that our richness as a people is expressed in how well we see beyond our fears, how well we direct our young, how well we listen to the wisdom of our elders, and how well we remember the achievements of our ancestors. Throughout our history, these questions have been asked: Where do I stand? Who do I stand with? Who stands with me? Many of history's accomplishments have been achieved by individuals standing together, but in many situations, one individual standing alone has made the difference.

Many of us have forgotten the events that make up our history. Slavery, torture, lynching, and segregation are elements of our history in which our inhumanity toward each other was painful, hateful, and accepted. The Holocaust shows us how one man's misguided thoughts and actions affected many innocent people. Other horrific incidents in history include the seizure of Native Americans' lands for settlements and the placement of Japanese Americans in internment camps. These are all actions that must not be repeated in this country or in any other country. All of these events have components of hate and betrayal embedded within them, and we continue to perpetuate them in our society today. We have forgotten the cost of lives, the shame, and the impact of these events. These are but a few of the many events that reflect negatively on us and show that we still have much to learn, although we see ourselves as a freedom-loving and compassionate country. But we forget that we are also a country that cannot always be trusted, just like any other country.

It took people from many walks of life to build and to create what we now call America. Our ancestors all came from different parts of the world, bringing with them their talents and gifts, which created a diverse population and enriched the tapestry of the American landscape for generations. Freedom was something that many had to fight for in America, and many continue to do so today. Many died with the hope that life would be better for others. America is a great country because of our diverse contributions, not because we believe we have conquered our destructive behavior. Our success as a country depends on all of us as a people believing in a vision of hope and creating possibilities that we can all share in. Only then can we be proud to say "We the people" and truly mean we the people. "We the people" needs to encompass not only those who hold power in our country but also those who are the grassroots of our country.

What children of color learn from these negative images in our history is that it is better to be someone other than themselves. I believe that every child must be a wanted child, and we as a country must make sure that children of color see themselves with potential and value. It is essential that all children know that it is important for them to be who they are and not yearn to be someone else in order to have their potential recognized, to belong, or to escape being bullied by peers. For many children and their families, poverty and education continue to be obstacles to achieving the American dream. Poverty and education also continue to be instrumental in deferring the dreams of children in other countries.

Somehow, because we are Americans, we want to believe that we have conquered the obstacles that many in our population continue to experience but that are not discussed on the nightly news. Whether it is due to violence from guns or violence from those who are sworn to protect us, people continue to suffer, sometimes in silence. I believe that remembering the positives and the negatives of our history can help us as a country to be better in words and deeds, if we truly want to be. Our children are watching us; what are we teaching them? The idea must be to build a more honest and compassionate society using the richness of our differences and the power of our commonalities to improve our society and not to destroy it for our children and grandchildren.

In America too many of us have died with unanswered dreams of a better tomorrow, a tomorrow in which economic, political, and social freedoms for all are realized. Many of us have attempted to embrace the American dream, but in the process, we have given up our identity and consequently our souls because we believed that this was required to belong, to be an American. Little did we know that much, much more would be required of us, and the American dream would continue to elude us because there are those among us who believe that they get to choose who is American, who is patriotic, and who the enemy is. This image of who has power and who does not is displayed in our newspapers, on nightly news broadcasts, and on radio stations every day without regard for anything except the number of people who watch or read each day.

In our history of the past and present, we have chosen to forget the stories of those who struggled for acceptance in the face of fear, terror, and death. This struggle continues today with individual and group hate. We must not forget that before 9/11, mass numbers of people were slaughtered on American soil, and this was done by Americans. Is it possible that America could be called a terrorist country? I believe that arrogance and privilege can leave us all blind to the pain we inflict on ourselves and others, and this pain does not come only from the Klan, militia groups, or other hate groups.

I believe that we cannot survive as a people or a country if we believe that we are separate from each other or if one group believes that it holds the moral compass for all of us and continues to practice exclusion of other groups. We also cannot survive when war and death are not seen as acts of supremacy in which we are all fatally wounded, but are instead seen as the acts of liberators of an oppressed people. We have forgotten that we have many times in our history been the oppressors. These facts continue to be very evident today, and women and girls of color must remember and bear witness to what is truth and what is an illusion.

We must remember that we as a country have a history of killing our leaders and enslaving our people while professing freedom and liberty. We continue to feed hatred, which is called many names by many different people. It is time that we as a country turn the spotlight on ourselves and examine what is killing us. I have heard it said many times that we as a people have come a long way but still have a long way to go. The reality of this statement will not change unless we as women and girls of all races make it our priority to change it. We are the remedy, and we are the ones who must stand and say that it is not acceptable to advocate for the destruction of any people anywhere. Extremist groups and extremist ideologies are designed to separate and to create a "them and us" attitude of superiority, which is an illusion about who we really are and what we can truly become as a people together.

In confronting the intersections of fear, hate, and racism and the lies that fear, hate, and racism are built on, women and girls can make a powerful difference. Making a difference begins with the grassroots, with you and with me. There are also many men who understand the value of being dependable allies to white women and girls, but they must also understand how to be dependable allies to women and girls of color.

Women and girls of color and white women and girls must stop perpetuating hate and violence as well. We must have confidence in our abilities to take positive actions in order to positively affect our lives. This means addressing and empowering the personal and political parts of our lives, as well as taking stands that may not be popular. We must strongly express our anger without apology and continue to speak truth to power. We must be courageous in the face of adversity and guard against attempts to silence each other overtly or covertly through stereotypes and hate speech, which are abusive acts that lead to destructive responses.

Women of color must learn ways to become better allies for each other in consciousness raising and in construction and implementation of policies that include rather than exclude us. Those who are our allies must learn ways they can become dependable allies in supporting the construction and implementation of policies that address women and girls of color as well as white women and girls through developing strategies of commitment, resistance, dialogue, change, and healing.

CHAPTER 15

Having the Conversation: What Are the Obstacles?

OUR ASSUMPTIONS, STEREOTYPES, AND MYTHS show us how our fears affect us and others, and they become institutionalized in the support of prejudice and misinformation. They also lead to a need to compete over limited resources, which can lead to discrimination and oppression.

The following are the major sources of prejudice in the United States:

- race
- gender
- class
- age
- sexual orientation
- language
- immigration status
- religion
- body image
- poverty

Barriers are perpetuated by individuals, schools, media, judicial systems, businesses, religions, workplaces, churches, and military institutions that overtly and covertly lead to acts of violence.

The most frequent triggers of violence in the world include the following:

- segregation
- enslavement
- internment
- scapegoating
- harassment
- hate crime
- name calling
- holocaust
- genocide
- massacre
- broken treaties
- economic exploitation
- displacement
- death

Prejudiced attitudes and beliefs such as the following lead to assumptions:

- superiority
- supremacy
- inferiority
- intolerance/disrespect
- ignorance

Perpetuation of misinformation leads to lies fueled by fear. Lies can, in turn, lead to the following:

- stereotypes
- omissions
- isolation
- hate speech

When we carry our unacknowledged pain, wounds, and sorrows internally, they sometimes get expressed externally in inappropriate ways through the following:

- denial
- fear
- blame
- shame
- mistrust
- exclusion
- anger
- powerlessness
- hopelessness
- guilt
- confusion
- hate
- violence

We must also ask ourselves how these expressions affect our mental, emotional, physical, and spiritual health in our everyday living, as well as in our everyday interactions with others. The drums are calling for us to return to the heart by remembering the well and the healing waters within.

CHAPTER 16

Having the Conversation: Therapy and Race

THROUGH THERAPY WE CAN DEVELOP a clear picture of who we are and discard the false images of ourselves supplied by others. I realize that there will always be people filled with anger and hate who are not willing to see beyond their anger and hate, but I continue to work for possible openings.

As a therapist who happens to be a woman of color and also a social activist who interfaces with clients in my professional life, I am always amazed at how much of a role race plays for clients who may be experiencing very severe difficulties. Either they bring some fragment of black history into the therapy session to ease into comfort for themselves, or they never return to sessions.

I have been blamed by clients for their not returning and have been blamed by my employer for the client leaving. But many clients have stayed in therapy with me and have gained benefits and knowledge for themselves through working with me, and I have gained benefits through working with them. For a time I would ask clients if they would have any difficulty working with a black therapist, but I have discontinued this practice. I know that there are white therapists who don't assume that a client of color would have difficulty working with them, so they never raise the topic of race with their clients.

In many places where I have worked, diversity and multicultural competency are expounded, but racism continues to rear its head unnoticed or, often, noticed but not addressed. In some places of employment, I have made the decision to stay to myself and not share personal or professional feelings or thoughts with others, because I believed that it was safer. Many times I feel out of step with those I work with because of this belief, but I attempt to keep an open heart by not allowing my concerns and emotions to take over. I find that I can practice this most of the time, but sometimes I fail.

I believe that multicultural competency and diversity are a set of policies that the workplace, agency, institution, or organization expounds but don't actually follow. I believe that multicultural competency and diversity must be practiced honestly, openly, and on a daily basis by all members in the workplace, agency, institution, or organization to be culturally effective.

In order for policies on multicultural competency and diversity to work, individuals must have a sense of self, with a desire to communicate, engage, and negotiate across multicultural and multiracial landscapes openly and honestly. They also need a willingness to ask questions, to listen, to be patient, and to exhibit an acceptance of multicultural and multiracial differences. Furthermore, they must strive to understand how systematic injustice and privilege in the workplace, institution, or organization can foster a "them and us" environment. In this toxic type of environment, failing to speak up for others, using stereotypical language, making offensive jokes or comments, denying another's history, and scapegoating can all encourage a sense of mistrust, anger, internal oppression, and powerlessness.

When the woman and social-activist parts of me begin to surface, the social justice juices rage within me, but I know that in order to be heard, I must pick and choose my words carefully, or I will be labeled an angry black woman, a bitch, a troublemaker, or an incompetent or insubordinate employee. The expectation is that I am to grin and bear it or find another position. I feel as if the woman-of-color part of me has been invisible to the clients I have served and the places where I have been employed. What they see are their stereotypes, assumptions, perceptions, and expectations, not me.

I realize that sometimes being a woman of color means withstanding criticism and being able to see what others may not see or feel but continuing to stand with dignity, even though there are moments when I fall. This also means having the ability to do whatever job I am doing with integrity and not becoming the victim or victimizer; this, I believe, is my contribution to myself, to my clients, and to the places where I have been employed.

I keep this motto at the forefront of my thinking, whether I am in a therapy session with a client or interacting with others on various levels of my everyday living: I have control over understanding myself and doing my best—and not over anyone or anything outside of myself—and this is my grace and strength. The only difficulty with this motto is that I expect this of others also, which is not realistic.

> *I have control over understanding myself and doing my best—and not over anyone or anything outside of myself—and this is my grace and strength.*

Having the Conversation: Sharing the Journey

MY PERSONAL JOURNEY BEGAN, AND has continued, with spending time thinking about what I want rather than what I don't want related to assumptions, stereotypes, and myths that I carry about myself, as well as what others carry about me.

My journey begins with me taking the following steps:

- showing honor and respect for myself and being present with others
- expressing fully who I am through presence and communication
- not allowing others' views or fears to stop my voice or passion
- not allowing others to dictate my behavior or who I am

I realize that if I listened to the world outside myself, I would continue to feel anger and frustration toward the world and the people in it.

I continue to grow in my attempts to change this scenario in the following ways:

- by setting limits and boundaries
- by saying what I mean and doing what I say
- by standing behind my actions
- by telling the truth without blame or judgment

- by remembering to validate and to acknowledge myself
- by being conscious of who I allow into my personal life

I have begun to focus more on my internal needs and wants, as well as on the external energy around me, through these actions:

- by paying attention to what has heart and meaning in my life
- by exploring my purpose, my dreams, my talents, and the resources available to me
- by staying grounded at the times when I feel like a plant that has been uprooted from her soil

By focusing on the external energy around me, I have begun to realize that the energy from our violent acts, as well as the energy from our abusive and hate-filled language, lingers very heavily among us in our homes, our communities, our churches, the workplace, and our institutions of learning.

I am learning that healing the wounds of the past and present begins with me, and that it will take compassion, patience, awareness, responsibility, and action from me to heal these wounds. I am also learning that hate and anger are not the cure for what ails us as a people or as a country—love is.

I am making healing connections with people who honor and respect who I am without question and whom I honor and respect in return. I recommend that you, too, connect with these types of people:

- people who are willing to find common ground in celebrating and communicating the contributions of all our people
- people who are willing to support each other in spite of the fears and stereotypes that we have learned about each other
- people who want to demonstrate the richness of our individual cultures, languages, and ways of being in the world through honoring the right of each of us to exist through respect, love, wisdom, and dignity

Women's history is filled with many courageous women who have fought against oppression in support of themselves and others in attempts to find common ground. Our history books may not tell us this, but we must remember that women and girls of color are also part of American history and have made enormous contributions and sacrifices to make this world a better place for all of us. Here are some of the ordinary heroes you will not read about in history books:

- women taking care of their families while also taking care of other women's families
- women who every day faced danger, disrespect, and betrayal in order to provide food, clothing, and shelter for their families

We may hear about the most famous women, but there are women who put their lives on the line every day and receive no reward or recognition for what they do. If our lives are to have meaning and value, we must reach deep into ourselves and bring forth the essence that is a part of each of us, as well as our connections to each other.

You may well ask why I bring up the past, opening old wounds. And I will say to you that I bring up the past so I will not forget, so we will not forget, the sacrifices, the losses, and the contributions made in our name. By acknowledging and healing the pain, the wounds, and the sorrows from the past and present, we can begin again—from a place of hope and compassion rather than from a place of fear.

In telling our stories, we become more conscious. We establish relationships with our past and present that are more open and accepting. Through telling our stories, we learn about the experiences, concerns, and cultures of another. We form relationships with each other that seek to understand our commonalities and our differences and to understand that our commonalities can be greater than our differences.

CHAPTER 18

Having the Conversation: And Asking Ourselves the Questions

As WOMEN AND GIRLS OF color and as white women and girls, we must ask ourselves the following questions. It is important to ask these questions in a culturally competent manner, because no matter what our interactions are, we carry into them our stereotypes, our myths, our assumptions, and our misinformation about each other, but we don't talk about them. Instead, we often display them in our interactions with each other in positive and negative ways.

- How do I foster hate within myself that is destructive to my coming together with other women on social and political issues?
- How do I deal with issues of difference, such as race, age, sexual orientation, gender, sexism, religion, disability, language, class, immigration, and ethnicity?
- Do I encourage women to celebrate their culture, traditions, and ethnicity, or do I encourage women to hide these parts of themselves?
- How do I perpetuate images of hate that I see in society today?
- What can I learn about the history of hate that will help me to be more sensitive and healing in my interactions?
- How can I use dignity, respect, and sensitivity in working with other women?
- How can I clearly look at the issues that face all women, particularly women who are not like me?

- How do privilege, skin color, beauty, sex, value, sexual orientation, ways of speaking, disabilities, age, culture, language, body image, class, religion, gender, and sexism play out in society's views of women and in my relationships?
- How can I become a better ally for myself and for other women?
- Do my words and actions bring peace and comfort to myself and others, or do they bring gossip, pain, and confusion?
- Am I open to learning that our experiences are not always in black and white but are also in many shades of gray?
- Am I open to seeing how gossip, collusion, manipulation, competition, and self-destructive expressions destroy us?
- How do I perpetuate violence, abuse, and hate?
- How do I deal with issues of difference and attempt to understand others, or is it every woman for herself?

What can I learn about the history of hate that will help me to be more sensitive and healing in my interactions with others?

CHAPTER 19

Having the Conversation: Women of Color Addressing Terrorism in America

ELECTING THE FIRST BLACK PRESIDENT in US history has tapped into many Americans' greatest fears and insecurities and allowed the racism that continues to grow in America to rear its ugly head, reminding us that no matter how much we think we have advanced, we still have a lot to learn. We must continue to confront the intersections of fear, hate, and racism, as well as the lies that fear, hate, and racism are built on.

Many who came to America seeking religious and political freedom are now practicing the oppression and terror that they escaped. Those who were brought to American in irons and chains, as indentured servants, and to work the railroads became the targets of hate-filled laws and hate-filled people. Many of us have forgotten that we are a nation of immigrants, except for the Native American, whose lands were taken. Many of us continue to struggle with laws that do not see us or understand us and, in many cases, don't care to.

As a country, we take pride in the democratic achievements and struggles for independence in America, but we must also address the inhumane past and present of our history. We must address how our past and present history scapegoats, blames, ignores, denies, and victimizes many of our citizens. As a country and as a people, we have terrorized and denied freedoms for many of our citizens, but we don't want to be called terrorist or racist or held accountable for the injustices of our history. Those who perpetrate terrorism want to be able to deny that they are terrorist or racist but continue to terrorize and dominate others.

We know that history is currently written with omissions, distortions, and deletions that give only half a picture of our entire history. We include only the parts of our history that don't make us feel uncomfortable. Our history must include the entirety of all our citizens' contributions—the events we take pride in and the events that cause us to rethink our humanity. This will then be a truthful account to all our children of what has really taken place in our history and in their history, as well as what we must do to improve individually and collectively as a country.

In addressing the injustices of the past, we can begin to change the injustices of the present. Here is a short list of some of the past injustices that we must address:

- the hardships of individuals who fled England for religious freedom
- the uprooting of Native Americans and the taking of their lands
- the practice of selling African Americans as property
- the Protestant mistreatment of the first Irish immigrants
- the exploitation of Chinese Americans who were brought to America to work on the railroads for low wages
- anti-Jewish sentiment in America, as well as discrimination toward Mexicans and Spanish-speaking individuals
- the emergence of the Klan
- the placement of Japanese Americans in internment camps
- antigay and antilesbian sentiment
- the continuing hostility between ethnic groups
- increases in gun violence
- restrictions on voters' rights and women's reproductive rights
- disparities in incarcerations
- police brutality in communities
- increases in militias
- hostility toward immigrants

We must also not forget to address the hostilities toward Barack Obama, our first African American president, and to give voice to what these hostilities really represent.

We cannot ignore these events in our history. We carry the energy and the memories of these events within us, and they cannot be rationalized away. We must be accountable and hold others accountable. We must be outraged when violence and terrorism happen, and we must give voice to this outrage. And we must admit that terrorism exists in America and that we as a people use it against each other. "We the people" must include all the people.

> *We can all drink from the well of life and partake of the potential nourishment that the healing waters provide. There is no need to have those who can drink and those who must stand by and look on with an unquenched thirst. Change comes when we are willing to look within ourselves, ask the tough questions and not abandon or lie to ourselves in the process. We can change, and we can improve, and it begins with you and me.*

MISSION OF WOMEN AS ALLIES:

Women As Allies is a nonprofit organization whose mission is to bring together women and girls of color with those who are our allies to create opportunities for dialogue, networking, healing, and action. The organization also strives to build relationships of compassion, trust, and hope that will bring about an increase in individual, collective, and universal consciousness on social justice issues, as well as on issues that involve our everyday experiences as women and girls.

Women As Allies realizes that in order to bring about change, we must be the instruments of that change. We believe that through our reverence for all women and humanity, we take responsibility for the problems that affect us, form relationships that are supportive and life affirming, make private and public choices for ourselves, and place trust in our abilities to change what hurts us.

We end where we began, with women and girls who are committed to making a difference within themselves, within their community, and within the world.

CHAPTER 20

Sharing Words of Inspiration, Hope, and Compassion

THIS IS A COLLECTION OF poems and reflections that encourage women and girls to never give up on our hopes and dreams as we work together in understanding and accepting our individual histories and commonalties.

Sharing

Through sharing our experiences,

we uncover the illusions that

we carry, and empower ourselves.

With conscious action, the

unconscious is revealed, and

we can bring about change for

ourselves and for others.

Our position is justice for all women,

but the words "all women" must

include and recognize women and girls of

color, our concerns, and our experiences.

Compassion

Women have the ability to be

compassionate individuals,

to understand the cycles of life, to

be mothering, and to attend to home

and hearth, but we must also embrace our

fears. Our growth as women and girls

depends on it.

Possibilites

In opening our hearts, possibilities emerge. We open to the mystery, beauty, and abundance that can be found in ourselves and others. This can be a crossroads for decision making and change with wisdom that comes from the heart.

Change

"Change" is a frightening yet powerful word. We go through many changes involving our emotions, yet we forget to honor the process. Exercising patience without blame or judgment can be a very healing and changing process.

Power

Our relationships with each other are
sometimes destructive and self-serving
instead of being ones of gentle power.
We can accomplish much when we
are no longer willing
to be victims or to victimize.

Trust

If women are to work together on issues

that concern us, we must form

relationships where we show respect for

each other. One important ingredient

needed in forming a relationship

of respect is trust.

Opportunity

Finding ourselves in situations that ask us to
step outside the norm, to be
uncomfortable, and to take responsibility
for that discomfort without guilt, blame,
or judgment of self or another offers an
opportunity to open our hearts and minds.

Our Stories

In telling our stories, we become more conscious. We establish relationships with our pasts and presents that are more open and accepting. Through telling our stories, we learn about the experiences, concerns, and cultures of others. We form relationships with each other that seek to understand our commonalities and our differences and to build on both.

Relationships

The question we must ask is, How do we form quality relationships with ourselves that are replicated in quality relationships with others, our families, our organizations, our workplaces, our communities, and our world?

Connections

As women and girls, we carry the seeds of the past, present, and future. What will be the cost to us if we ignore each other's tears and sorrows through fear, jealousy. ignorance, criticism, and misunderstanding? If we deny our connections to each other and kill the spirit that we each bring from all the corners of the world, what will be the cost to us, to our children, to our men, to our world, and ultimately to ourselves?

Women As Allies

Our work is not to inflate or deflate ourselves. It is to shed what does not work in our lives; to balance the feminine; to release anger, fear, and jealousy; to honor the right of each of us to be; to make space for others to enter our lives; to respect the children of others as much as our own; to believe that all accomplishments are important to society; to let go of what does not serve us; to acknowledge and to bear witness to what is real and not an illusion. Women As Allies believes that women can change the world, but we must also be willing to change ourselves and to understand that each and every

individual has a right to walk in the world

and to be treated with dignity and respect.

Women Know the Way

Women know the way. We know how to care for each other. We know how to not allow another to fall. We know how to look behind and ahead for each other. We know how to ensure that none of us is left behind. We know how to hold hands and trust. We know how to look into each other's eyes and find a way through our fears, tears, losses, and pain. We know how to leave blame, judgment, and competitiveness behind. We know how to touch the deepest love and the deepest wound. We know how to use love and hope. We know how to be the lights in our homes when fear appears. We know how to value the beauty in all things.

Let us not be afraid to walk together, although the road can be long, dusty, and paved with many detours. Let us not be distracted by the pebbles and stones that can trip us up along the way. Let us remember to learn each other's stories and promise never to forget. Let us remember the courage and strength of our mothers, grandmothers, and great-grandmothers. Let us not be afraid of each other. We know each other, and we know how to move beyond our fears. We have taken this journey before,
and each day we begin again.

Value

There are those who may feel that I have no value, but my value comes from within me and not from outside of me.

In My Mother's Name

My mother carried me in her arms, she held
me close to her breast, she knew what I
would need to survive, she knew as many
before her knew—mothers, grandmothers,
and great-grandmothers—that to be a
woman or girl in this time would take
confidence, courage, and wisdom.
She knew nothing would be given to me,
and I would have to find my way alone,
unprotected, and unseen.
She knew I would need her smell,
her touch, her strength, her voice, and
her look to keep me strong,
because one day she would be gone,
and I would have to remember.

Images

As I continue to grow in a world that is very confused and torn, I realize that as a woman, I must continue to come into myself with the hope of continually defining who I am with my wants, my needs, my sorrows, and my joys in this society. I must decide what the legacy is that I want to leave for my grandchildren and how I can do this in a clear and concise way. I believe that one way I can do this is by becoming very clear about my strengths and weaknesses. In order to do this, I must look at some of the images I hold of myself. As I look at these images, I can decide what and how I want to project myself in the world. Then I must affirm the positive images rather than the negative ones. When I affirm the positive images, I leave clear examples of who I am. Then there is no confusion for myself or others. I must also continue to see that what I do as a woman affects others. Therefore, having positive images of myself can help bring clarity into my relationships with others and with myself. The dream is that I learn and learn—with each new day I learn. I learn to see myself as a woman who is vital, positive, and important and to not embrace the images that others hold of me, whether negative or positive.

My Father's Wisdom

My father always said to my sisters,

brothers, and me as we were growing up

that we should always remember who we

are and where we came from

and to treat ourselves and others with

dignity and respect, even if dignity and

respect are not given to us in return.

I carry my father's words with me always,

even at times when his words are hard to follow.

My Son's Smile

My son's smile, his gray-green eyes, and the
quietness of his voice. I remember the
strong determination of his heart that
filled the need to take care of his family,
although his heart gave out too soon.
His legacy lives on in his children, in his
family, and most of all in his brother.

Mom Two

Mom Two never gave up on me, and she pushed me to be better than I believed that I could be. There were times when I was angry with her, but she never abandoned me, and sometimes she also pushed back. Mom Two nurtured and guided me through the self-discovery years of my life. She gave me the tools to take risks and to make decisions for myself. She encouraged me to find the answers to the questions that troubled me rather than to ignore them because of my fears. She encouraged me to embrace the world and to know that she would be there when I returned home.

She always had my back.

Listening

Our richness as a people is expressed in how
well we see beyond our fears, how well we
direct our young, and how well we listen
to the wisdom of our elders.

Tapestry of Life

The Fulfillment of Hopes
and Dreams Continues to Be Woven
through the Tapestry of Life.

Divisions

Women scholars have placed the spotlight on the divisions between white women and women of color, as well as divisions between women of color. What will we do to mend these divisions?

Friends, Sisters, Allies

Friends, sisters, and allies weaving a dream through the tapestry of life. Letting us know that no matter what, we count and our achievements matter. Encouraging us to insist that our aspirations be treated with dignity and respect. Assisting us in knowing that we are always deserving and good enough and not allow others to define who we are. Friends, sisters, and allies supporting us in knowing our worth and feeling safe, secure, and protected in this knowledge. Guiding us in knowing that empathy and compassion must always be a part of who we are and what we share with others. Letting us know that change is a constant in the tapestry of women's

and girls' lives and that

we must never give up on each other.

My husband and I

continue to be inspired

and to dream the dream that we started in 1966.